VIVID LINES

Kenneth Lee

Webster Falls Media™

Books · Films

www.WebsterFalls.com

© 2022 by Kenneth Lee

All Rights Reserved.

No part of this book may be reproduced in any form, including electronic, digital or mechanical means, without written permission of the author. Reviewers may quote brief passages in a review only.

Published by Webster Falls Media LLC
Wallace, N.C. · Burbank, CA

www.websterfalls.com

First Edition

ISBN (paperback): 978-0-9816872-8-5
Library of Congress Control Number: 2021952938

Printed in the USA

Solstice

Pollen still falling,
warmer we passed the corner,
to the other side of the season;
ever following our reason.
For the things we should
is what we could.
But, never our reality.
Loving you will always be
my greatest tragedy.

Kenneth Lee

Roadrunner

These are the days
to do anything we want.
There is never a better time than now.
Those wasted moments should be spared.
I won't be tied down till 30.
A decade is what we have.
I've learned thru their mistakes.
I am not one to rush my life away.
So, pick a place and let's go, cause' I'm
bored.

Kenneth Lee

Fire for You

You're one of those clouds
That pass over the sun a moment,
To help me catch a breath of fresh air.
And yet —— you seem to be the sun, too
Warm and fiery red.
Just what I needed from a brittle winter.
The color and breeze
is what I've been begging for,
And you give me all that I ask.

Kenneth Lee

Questionable

Making you wonder
is my favorite thing after all.

Kenneth Lee

Wet

You have
the sweetest water.
I'm begging for you
to drip on my tongue,
Quench my thirst.
The desert
no place
To deny my refreshment.
The taste
I long for.
I long for you.
While in this vastness
that we reside,
Refresh me
I beg of you
rain on me.

Kenneth Lee

Honeybee

You flew right into my lips
where you should have never been.
It wasn't the first time.
It will be the last.

Your name does you justice
for the pain you solicit.
The sweet words that make you
are nothing but a lie.

Something sounds sweet
till proven otherwise
and the stinger you left
made me realize
it was true.

Kenneth Lee

Morgan

I could never forget when I was a boy with you,
down by the lake.
You'd keep me up all night
in the water by the arcade.
I'll never forget how those moments felt.
I think of those days often.
Nothing is the same.
We will never be.
Those days
I sure have grown to love.

I drove by your old place the other day actually.
The palm had doubled and so did my heart,
for the place
you once lived
and I loved.

Kenneth Lee

Propagation

Let me take you in the garden
to see what other than roses
I can make bloom.

Kenneth Lee

Dirty Sheets

I miss the sunlight on your face
in the morning;
sneaking a glimpse
at what I missed at night.
with what I'm missing more now.
If those hazel eyes opened
would my look upon thee
discourage them
to stay away?
Or fall all in
oblivion.

Kenneth Lee

Dutch Dreams

One afternoon I walked thru
our neighborhood
saving my breath,
to lose it in the smoke.

If I could feel those walls
I would be golden.
If I could see you
like I wanted to,
like I used to,
before you
had your best dreams come true,
I would be in my own.

Kenneth Lee

VIVID LINES

T

When I look back at your photographs,
trying to see someone I knew,
I'm revealed the image
of the love
that melted my heart
With the brightest sun leaving me
to harden around the smallest rock
in your gravel,
I see all the things I once loved.
I see all the things that made me feel at home.
You've changed
You scrape at my bones.
My love means nothing but a flattery
to pride yourself with your newfound life.

Kenneth Lee

Teeth

You don't know
what it means
to make me smile.

I'd do it all.

Let me prove it to you.

Kenneth Lee

Botanophobia

Green vines entangle me,
the vines of your love I once knew
I tried reaching for the pocketknife
and you gripped onto me.
Wanting my life, but not who I was.
Taking away the power I've always had.
Now trapped in your forest,
I pray for someone to help
take me away from this love
I wrongfully deserve.
Their thorns laid their mark
and the only mark I left
was the sap dripping underneath
what was to expect.
Something will always grow.
Thorns or tulips you gamble,
or maybe something sweeter.
A cherry tree?
No, I wouldn't be that lucky.
Not a million years.
Just a million vines
to grow into.

Sirens

I saw your hand
 reaching out of the water.
You reached for the sun and the air
Gasping for a breath.
With only oceans around,
far from the land,
I knew I had to act fast
before the hand
was like the rest of you,
ready to sink to the sand.
I passed the waves until I was almost to you
when a fin marked you.
I knew I'd have to get you away
from those sharp teeth and sirens
before they possessed you.
But what possessed me
was my action of flight.
And before I knew it
you had me strung like a kite.
You were the siren and shark.
You brought me to the dark.
And you showed me a false image
to get me here.
You took me to the bottom of the ocean
where I should have left you all along.

Kenneth Lee

What a beautiful hand I had seen.
What a projected thought that was
a damsel in distress,
more like a thirsting vulture
for the blood of men.
I won't forget.
How could I forget
my last moments.

VIVID LINES

Kenneth Lee

VIVID LINES

K

I want to write on your body
with the capital letter of my name
so they know you belong to me.
So they won't touch your body
but you'll just wash it in the rain.
Say it's not worth a stain.
Guess that'd be using your brain.

Kenneth Lee

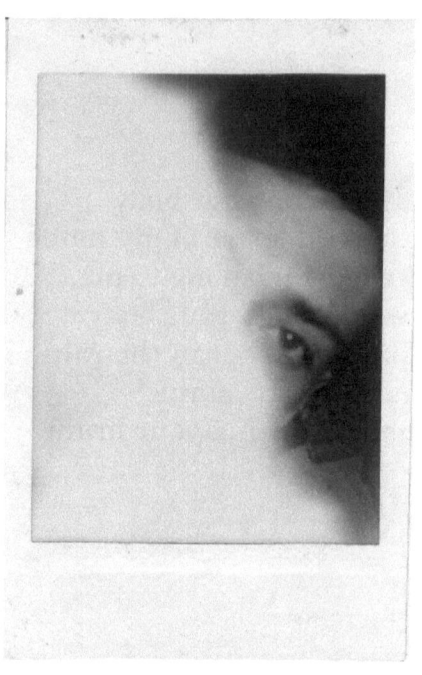

Falling

It's never easy
to let you in.
But I do and it always hurts.
I do —— I never learn.
I tend to fall at the beginning,
Whirling, twirling and spinning
with my eyes bloodshot and heart shaped.
I think I'd learn to be rigid
after each fall.
I hit the ground,
falling to pieces.
It's never easy
putting myself back together.
It's never easy
acting as I don't weather.
With a soul like mine
I deserve more.
With the heart I have
it's an open door.
For heartache and love to come pass by,
never staying over a night.
Belittling me.

Kenneth Lee

Ball & Chain

You tell me my ways should change,
but whose life am I living?
Tell me my ways should change.
Hope you're kidding.
You live your own life.
I'm done playing by your rules.
I live my own life.
with no pride to lose.
Don't live my life.
Let me choose.
Guide me.
Don't ride me.
That's a battle you'll lose.

Kenneth Lee

Eye See You

I saw you
lie to me.

I dare you.

Kenneth Lee

Witchy Woman

I haven't heard from you in years.
I'd been waiting for the day
you'd return.
But the only way
is to watch you burn.

Kenneth Lee

Widow

You told me if I let her see my teeth
she would write my name in her web for
me to fall into.
I couldn't help the way you made me
smile.
I bared them in the moment.
I was happy for a second,
until I was falling in her cobwebs.
And she crawled in my eye

Kenneth Lee

Aphrodite

The only person
I don't mind coming & going.
I see you like blue moon,
something like Hades
waiting for her,
If Helios didn't spill
it'd be you,
trapped forever.
Demeter will come when you're gone.
I won't be ready.
A trade of life
perhaps.
I remember
the shore after I left you,
crying for your touch,
melting in my tears.
You were worth spring and winter
and she was barely worth a day.

Kenneth Lee

Irony

The day I realized I loved you,
you no longer felt the same.
It's not my fault, neither yours.
No one to blame.

Kenneth Lee

Cheat

I missed being home,
and now I'm here with you.
Everything is different.
Something is new.
I thought about it hard.
I know I wasn't wrong.
Everything is different.
Something is gone.
I remember it perfectly
and then I forget.
There used it be love here.
Who flipped the switch?
How things change
is always
a mystery.
Feelings change.
Never our history.

Kenneth Lee

Oblivious

Who wants to be reminded of yesterday when it was that beautiful and effortless to be so happy and unaware of the never ending circumstances of your love and our life.

Kenneth Lee

Our Song

I thought I'd never hear those words
from another.
While wrapped up in a time
that seems forever.
But, I did and for a second it felt like I was
there again with you.
They never knew.
It wasn't the same.
We all make time for the things we want
and that's important to realize.
However, you won't learn unless you stop
trying.
It takes getting broken 100 times
to realize that and that's the sad truth.
But you'll still be the one I think of
when I hear those words
from our song
and that's not okay.
But no one will ever know.

Kenneth Lee

Secret

You whispered in my ear
like I was your secret.
Maybe I was.

Kenneth Lee

Autumn

The walls aren't warm anymore.
They're monochrome.
The paths we walked
overgrew where our feet stepped.
Running in the fields.
Riding alligators in the swamp
and living together
is no more,
My room is your room now.
The floors the same.
The memories are there.
We were mean. but the best pair
freckled year round.
Do you remember my hound?
Or, going fishing the first time?
Feeding the ducks with Papa?
Eating the cherries in the spring?
If I heard your young voice
my ears would ring
because that was yesterday.

Kenneth Lee

Knockout

Times wouldn't be this hard
if God didn't have a plan for me.
I'll roll thru the punches hoping to fall
gracefully.

Kenneth Lee

VIVID LINES

Lake Whore

Hearing those lines.
The beats we felt together
when they come on the stereo
It is one thing that gives me that feeling
knowing I was with you
Hearing those same words.
It will always make me happy
to know that there is meaning
in so much of each day.
Just hope you're doing okay.

Kenneth Lee

Lungs

I miss catching my breath
with you.

Kenneth Lee

Reaper

You never realize how good or bad
you have it until you are down,
needing someone to save you.

Kenneth Lee

2001 Second Avenue

Not many nights to worry
about the trees towering above.
The city I used to love
has passed by me
and I'm not ready for you or me to go.
This is the last time I'll have company
to enjoy the house with me.
Memories echo thru,
making it harder and sweeter to love.
The walls falling down.
But I'll never forget how it once stood.
Feeling the sunshine
I felt on the warmest days of my life.
I will always remember.
Or, so I hope.

Kenneth Lee

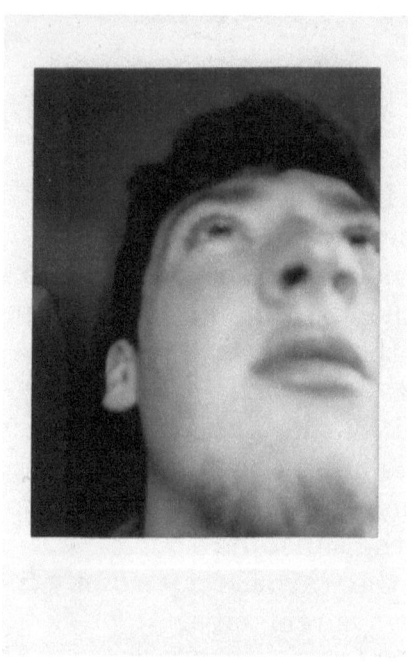

Novocaine

The things we used to do,
never going through
the what if's and when
we were caught in the wind.
Does that make you wonder?
It could be better.
It could be different.
if we changed the effort.
Don't make me the only one
thinking about what used to be,
cause baby that'd hurt.
But what doesn't?
Cause I haven't found the Novocaine
to numb myself since I started hurting.
Have you been hiding it from me?
Or did you hide it from yourself?

Kenneth Lee

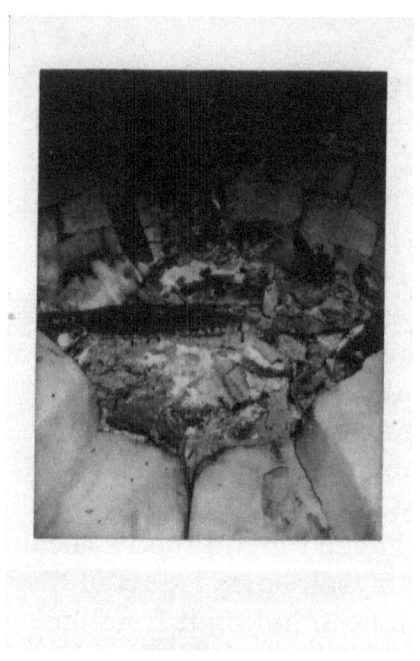

Green Blades of Summer

I was in the leaves
with a shoe between
You and me,
with a revolver and light thru my window
where I was on your mind.
I was shaking with the trees
wondering when you'd leave
so I could catch the warmth of the fire.
But you were here for justice.
My feet bleeding from spurs.
the hounds could smell me out
and I'd run even longer,
dripping burgundy
over the green blades of summer.

Kenneth Lee

Time Change

Everything gets cold in the winter
waiting for you to shine.
Shaking without your warmth.
That should be a crime.
I try to love December,
but I can only remember
it wasn't always so cold.
I guess you just stopped shining on me.

Kenneth Lee

Necessities

Left me with bad habits and unsatisfaction,
My trust, my goals, my love.
Lost within the smallest window.
I was searching and found what I wanted.
But at the end of the day, I had only what I needed.

Kenneth Lee

VIVID LINES

Fame

Tragedy in fame.
Only yourself to blame.
They'll love you forever.
Before you weather
fire and rain
is how it came.
I won't be the same.
Only myself to blame.

Kenneth Lee

Loss

What have we become,
if nothing but a memory

Kenneth Lee

Perception

You won't ever understand
when you ask and hear my words.
For it shows nothing to thee
if not put in my perspective.
They will never mean
what they are intended to.
I hope you would try on these shoes
and ask what has them this heavy?
For it's not your nature.
You never said it was so.

Kenneth Lee

Sweetheart

You were my special
part hanging by a
thread.
Even when
on a date I think of you
in my full-sized bed.

Kenneth Lee

Brickhouse

You couldn't wait any longer for me to leave and you to be gone.

Kenneth Lee

God Bless

Child of the king is who you are.
Be abundant in the pride of His name.
Do things to embrace Him.
Never neglect Him.
Even if hard to maintain
your days will be long.
If you sing your song in His name
He will shower you with His love.
He will shower you with His time.
Boast and pride yourself with
the glory He gives only to the one
truly loving Him.
Withdraw your resentment.
Show compassion
and watch the ways of your life change.
I've seen it more than once.
I'm begging to do the same.

Kenneth Lee

Hydroponic

I feel resolved.
I feel collected
when I hit you.

Kenneth Lee

Beachboy

I snuck out that night.
Got on the boat.
I was smoking.
Holding in
every
toke.

Kenneth Lee

Born to Die

Good things
never last forever.

Kenneth Lee

Polyurethane

Desolate body.
What makes you think
of me in a manner of mistake?
I will not tolerate.
You must be missing something up there.
Has there been a day for you in a lifetime?
That is something we all hope.
Some days never come.
While more have days of sun on their
cheeks,
I am bound to the calluses of hammer
and you,
while inhaling your tonics.
What a lucky bitch.
And me?
A damn fool.

Kenneth Lee

Allure

I was by the fire
waiting on you to warm me
when something unsettled me.
A far cry I had heard before.
I didn't tell anyone where I was going.
I followed the scream.
Until I was lost in the woods,
searching the sound.
You called for me.

Kenneth Lee

Citrus Veins

Vibrant yellow peel.
Very inviting.
Citric acid.
Burns enticing.
So sour. So sweet,
just as your heart.
If I cut it open
Would you be as tart?

Kenneth Lee

January

You're like a warm day in January.
Never where you're supposed to be.
Yet somehow,
you're exactly where I needed you.

Kenneth Lee

Worth

You deserved the world.
Just not mine.

Kenneth Lee

Hydrofluoric

I love you to pieces.
So, I sit and watch you dissolve.

Kenneth Lee

About Time

It took all the pain
to find all the things I've been searching
for.
This feeling is overwhelming.
Nothing better than now.

Kenneth Lee

Art Piece

You were a piece of art.
I just wanted to frame you.

Kenneth Lee

Rosacea

I've been turning red.
Better than blue.

Kenneth Lee

Mom

The Azalea still blooms.
Not in the way you'd expect either.
She waits until your birthday.
However, the beauty is admired
from someone new.
She's sure it blooms for her.
But we both know
it blooms for you.

Visit the author's website

www.KennethLeePoetry.com

Explore the work of other great authors

from Webster Falls Media

www.WebsterFalls.com

www.ingramcontent.com/pod-product-compliance
Lightning Source LLC
Chambersburg PA
CBHW032044290426
44110CB00012B/945

9780981687285